PENGUIN SPECIALS

Penguin Specials fill a gap. Written by some of today's most exciting and insightful writers, they are short enough to be read in a single sitting – when you're stuck on a train; in your lunch hour; between dinner and bedtime. Specials can provide a thought-provoking opinion, a primer to bring you up to date, or a striking piece of fiction. They are concise, original and affordable.

To browse digital and print Penguin Specials titles, please refer to **penguin.com.au/penguinspecials**

A Universe of One's Own

ANTONIA HAYES

For Josephine and Michael
(or as I like to call them, Mum and Dad)

PENGUIN BOOKS

UK | USA | Canada | Ireland | Australia
India | New Zealand | South Africa | China

Penguin Books is part of the Penguin Random House group of companies whose addresses can be found at global.penguinrandomhouse.com.

Penguin
Random House
Australia

First published by Penguin Random House Australia Pty Ltd, 2017

The essay 'A Universe of One's Own' was first written and performed as a Curiosity Lecture for the 2016 Sydney Writers' Festival

Copyright © Antonia Hayes, 2017

The moral right of the author has been asserted

All rights reserved. Without limiting the rights under copyright reserved above, no part of this publication may be reproduced, stored in or introduced into a retrieval system, or transmitted, in any form or by any means (electronic, mechanical, photocopying, recording or otherwise), without the prior written permission of both the copyright owner and the above publisher of this book.

Printed and bound in Australia by Griffin Press,
an accredited ISO AS/NZS 14001 Environmental
Management Systems printer.

ISBN: 9780143782490

penguin.com.au

MIX
Paper from
responsible sources
FSC® C009448

CONTENTS

Mother Tongue 1

Super Special #1 49

A Universe of One's Own 63

Mother Tongue

My mother never taught me her mother tongue. She was born on the island of Luzon, in Manila: the chief port and capital city of the Philippines. When she was eleven years old, she moved to Sydney to attend boarding school – so she speaks English with an Australian accent – but her first language is Tagalog. This was what my mother spoke with her own mother; its sounds were the music of her childhood, the rhythm of her first words, the murmurs of her earliest dreams. Tagalog is my mother's native language, but it has always felt foreign to me.

Tagalog is the mother tongue of over a quarter of the population of the Philippines and is spoken as a second language by the majority – almost 100 million people. One of the country's two official languages is Filipino, formed as a result of President Manuel Quezon's mandate to have a national language – in theory, Filipino is meant to be an amalgam of Tagalog and other languages of the Philippines but is basically purely Tagalog; there are hardly traces of other dialects in it. The other official language is English. But in a country containing more than 7000 islands, with nineteen major dialects, nearly everyone in the Philippines is a polyglot. Across the archipelago, the Filipino population speaks more than 175 living languages.

The word Tagalog, derived from *taga* and *ilog*, means 'river dweller'. The dialect was originally spoken by the Tagalog people, who lived along the rivers and streams that connect the waters of the volcanic basin of the Laguna Caldera and Sierra Madre mountain range to the mouth of Manila Bay. Manila is a watershed, built on the Valley Fault System, the volatile tectonic framework of uneasy strata that slips and slides below the metropolis. For me, Metro Manila is a metropolis in every sense of the word: in Greek, 'metropolis' means 'mother state'. My mother's city was constructed around a complex network of waterways: more than thirty tributaries flow within the urban area.

Marikina, Pasig, San Juan, Tullahan, Nangka, Ampid: these are the rivers of my maternal lineage, the waters from where my ancestry flows – the source. Sprung from these rivers, descended from river dwellers, but I don't speak their dialect. So I worry – am I where these currents stop moving? Where language is literally a barrier, a dam?

Mother tongue is called our arterial language, as though it lives inside our bodies and is carried by our blood. Half my genes are Filipino and, like my mother, I have dark hair and dark eyes. We share the same blood type, I have her cheekbones and mouth, but language isn't hereditary like antigens or bone structure. Tagalog was never written into my DNA. Then again, neither was English.

In my early childhood, my exposure to Tagalog came mostly through Ona, my maternal grandmother who still lives in Manila. She's too old to travel now – she just turned ninety-three – but when I was little, Ona visited us in Sydney at least twice a year. I call her Ona because when I was a baby, that was the noise that came out of my mouth when she was trying to teach me the Tagalog word for grandmother – *lola*. The name Ona stuck; I've never called my grandmother *lola*.

From the moment I started talking, our family created a new language: Tagalog overwritten with reinvented words. Ona spoke to me primarily in English, but taught me some basic Tagalog like *salamat* (thank you), *busog-na* (I'm full), *masarap* (delicious) and *puwit* (bum). I can count to ten and name my body parts; I know the colours and the days of the week. I still speak Tagalog like a two-year-old. For a long time, I've wondered why I never became fluent.

Childhood language acquisition has two distinct phases: passive (listening), then active (reproducing words and sounds). Babies first learn to talk by listening to the language spoken around them. My parents always spoke English with each other, and then with me. But Tagalog was often spoken around me as well. I've been listening to the language since I was in the womb. My grandmother and mother always talk to each other in Tagalog. All my life, the rhythms and cadences of their conversations in Tagalog have been a steady background thrum. So I hear its music. I recognise the language's patterns of stresses and glottal stops, and the tempo of its grammar. Like humming a familiar tune but not remembering the words, I've memorised Tagalog's melody without learning its lyrics. Just its notes and chords – I only know half the song.

During the active phase of language acquisition, infants start interacting: repeating what they've heard, reproducing the sounds and intonations of overheard language. I have vague memories of trying to repeat Tagalog words, to see how they might feel in my mouth, but I wasn't really urged to speak it.

From the beginning, my garbled attempts at Tagalog weren't corrected or encouraged by my mum or grandmother. They didn't let me play with it, as if their language was a toy that didn't belong to me. Words and phrases trickled into my ears, but because there wasn't enough interaction in Tagalog, I never moved past the passive stage of childhood language acquisition and into active fluency.

Neurolinguistic studies have shown how simply listening to a new language creates structures in the brain required to learn it – neural tissue develops automatically when we hear a language's combinations of sounds. Scaffolding for Tagalog exists inside my brain. Listening to those background conversations between my mother and grandmother created a skeleton of neural structures. But this is only cartography, not the complete landscape. To me, Tagalog is a street directory with nameless streets, a map without legend and scale. I can get my bearings but I can't navigate or direct. Following isn't the same as understanding and manoeuvring – I cannot masterfully steer the ship.

When I was a child, I used to believe that my mother – and grandmother – simply didn't want me to speak Tagalog; that they kept their shared language secret from me on purpose. Mum had no desire to teach me; I never understood why. In my kid logic, I figured that since I was only half-Filipino, maybe my diluted brain could only learn half the language. Or perhaps if I couldn't speak Tagalog, it'd be easier for them to talk about me, not just behind my back but in front of my face. Whenever they did, though, I always understood – my name's the same in every tongue.

Sometimes my grandmother yelled at my mother in Tagalog, and my mum would storm out of the room with glistening eyes. She'd sit in the dark, by the windowsill, and light a cigarette, coils of smoke unfurling from its glowing tip. When I was old enough to notice how upset she was, I'd ask Mum about their fight and what was wrong. 'Nothing,' she'd say blankly, continuing to stare out the window. 'You wouldn't understand.'

She was right. I didn't.

So I started to think Tagalog wasn't a language I wanted to speak anyway, if it meant getting upset and having fights. All that shouting and crying, the repeated syllables of its inflected verbs pounding like a beating war drum, its staccato pulse firing vowels like machine-gun rounds. To my ears, Tagalog began sounding caustic, nasty and cruel. Filled with high-pitched shrieks and whines. My mother's mother tongue was the language of arguments, of tears, of hurt feelings. Why would I want to be fluent in pain?

Later, when I was older and started to argue with my mother like she argued with my grandmother, I realised that we can hurt each other's feelings no matter which language we speak.

My mother's English is the opposite of broken – it's intact, perfect, unmatched. She's a polyglot: as eloquent in English as in her mother tongue, fluent in French and Spanish, can recite *Beowulf* in Anglo-Saxon. But this is about more than proficiency. Her command of English isn't just immaculate; my mother's linguistic dexterity is about as good as it gets. When she did her Higher School Certificate, she came first in 3 Unit English in New South Wales, beating everyone else in the state. She studied English Literature at Oxford University, attended the same college as Iris Murdoch and Margaret Thatcher. My mum wrote scripts for TV shows: *A Country Practice*, *Lift-Off*, *Home and Away*. She was a literary critic, and she's better read than anybody I know. But mostly, my mother worked as an editor, of books – which brought an interesting dynamic to our parent–child relationship since all I've ever wanted to do was write them.

We speak about language as though it's liquid: total immersion, absorption rates, watered-down descriptions. The word fluent comes from the Latin verb *fluere* – 'to flow' – and while our conversations might flow, we can also be deep in them. Words burst out of us, stories splash across front pages, complaints flood our inboxes. Writers get blocked, voices are drowned out. Rivers have mouths, communication has channels, consciousness has streams. We gush with enthusiasm, we spill our secrets, we brim with ideas. Babies babble like brooks and gurgle like creeks. We can have outpourings of feeling, or bottle them up.

I was a porous child – a sponge, a mimic. I regurgitated everything I heard. I'd soak words up then spit them out. I liked figuring out how to blend them together and what happened when they split.

In our family folklore, all the frequently repeated stories about my childhood involve me imitating an adult. How I called stained-glass windows 'superbs' because this was the word my father said out loud when he gazed at them in awe. How, when I had the measles at eighteen months, I asked the doctor, 'What's happening to the baby?' repeating the question my worried parents had already asked. How, as a two-year-old, I pointed to the sunset and said it was 'the golden bough on the *horizman*' (copying my dad again). How I greeted people when I was a toddler in Switzerland by yelling '*Bourgeois!*' instead of '*Bonjour!*' (another word almost picked up from Dad). I didn't really know what I was saying, but I guess I had something to say.

Words intrigued me, from the moment I discovered what they were. But this preoccupation felt visceral too: my childhood relationship with words was sensory. My eyes saw the world in words first, shapes and colours next. My ears heard speech before other sounds; my nose smelled phrases before scents; my hands touched nouns before they felt objects; my tongue tasted adjectives before flavours. I seriously used to believe that language was like taste, sight, sound, touch and smell – that we had a word-sense.

From as early as four years old, I was curious about English's patterns and rules too. I wanted to unravel how language worked and why, and learn the stories behind its systems and structures. Luckily my mum was an English scholar and understood linguistics.

'Mummy,' I'd say, 'if two mouses are mice, how come two houses aren't called hice?'

'Back when people spoke Old English, instead of adding the letter "s" to the end of a word to make it plural, sometimes they changed a vowel instead. That's called an i-mutation,' my mum told me. 'We only use it for some words. One house, two houses. One mouse, two mice.'

'Then why isn't one ice cream,' I'd continue, 'called an ouse cream?'

Language may not be written into our DNA, but our capacity to learn it might be. Neurobiologists have identified a gene that correlates to language: the FOXP2 gene, which plays a key role in speech development and vocalisation.

My parents share a love of words, but I inherited my porosity for them from my dad. My father has a natural ear for language and can easily mimic an accent, although he didn't grow up bilingual like my mother. I've learned almost as much Tagalog from my dad as from my mum, even though most of the Tagalog he knows is self-taught – absorbed through listening, gleaned meaning and osmosis. His brain is wired for language, I think. He loves listening to the radio, spoken word, poetry; he always hears language's music. So I couldn't talk about mother tongue without talking about my dad.

Adult input is an important factor in the linguistic development of children. Language acquisition is interactive; it involves both parent and child. Studies of parental speech patterns show how parents make special accommodations when they speak to their children. Linguists called this 'mother talk', the ideal learning language: grammatical, simple and repetitious, spoken in a slow and clear voice. As children grow older, the complexity of this 'mother talk' gradually increases with their grasp of language.

Mothers are tuned into their children, but this isn't unique to mothers. Men also modify their speech when addressing young children; they're just as sensitive as women to the language needs of kids. While some linguistics studies have shown variances in speech patterns between mothers (who rephrase instructions as questions more often) and fathers (who use more verbs in the imperative, expressing commands like 'come here!'), these slight differences are cultural, not biological. Those specific variations are not seen in studies of male day-care teachers' speech, which closely mirrors the language of their female day-care colleagues. Mother talk is father talk too.

My first language is my father's mother tongue: the English language, by way of Norfolk, Dorset, Somerset and Middlesex, England; and Fermanagh, Tyrone, Kildare and Cork, Ireland; then brought across oceans and seas to Australia. Anthony Rope, my fifth great-grandfather, left Portsmouth, England aboard *Alexander* – one of the eleven ships of the First Fleet – and sailed southwest across the Atlantic Ocean, then east via the Great Southern Ocean to Botany Bay. My English-speaking ancestors put their roots down in Windsor, Melbourne, Lismore, Cassilis, and finally Burwood, New South Wales.

Barrow, Avon, Thames, Hawkesbury, Yarra, Munmurra, Parramatta: these are the rivers of my paternal lineage, the other waters from where my ancestry flows – the second source. River settlers rather than river dwellers, their colonial ripples extending through the Empire.

So it was the sounds of English – in London, Lane Cove, Leura – that were the music of my childhood, the rhythm of my first words and the murmurs of my earliest dreams. Dad was often the one I mimicked when I tried to talk; I heard what he said, said what I heard. Both my parents taught me how to speak, but my mum is more introverted and quiet, while my dad is much more talkative and interactive. My primary learning language was 'father talk'.

When I speak, I sound a lot like my dad. Even though he has a much deeper voice, I share his accent and intonation and variety of vocal inflections. My younger sister sounds exactly like me; it's hard to differentiate us on the phone. While the shape and size of our vocal chords are probably similar, my sister and I don't have the same voice because we have the same larynx. We have different mothers – our common voice comes from Dad. Both of us listened to his intonations and inflections, which created the same scaffolding for our first language inside both our brains.

My relationship with language changed when my son was born. When I became a mother, my language became my child's mother tongue. But it wasn't that simple and straightforward with Julian. Listening to the sound of my voice did create structures in my son's brain, his English language neural tissue developing as I spoke. But he wasn't speaking back.

The word infant comes from the Latin *infans*, which means 'not speaking', so it wasn't unusual that baby Julian couldn't talk. As he grew into a toddler, his silence grew worrying. Julian struggled to access his scaffolding. The automatic framework of language constructed inside his brain seemed too big to scale, too high to conquer – just out of his reach.

At nineteen months old, my son was found to have significantly delayed language abilities, due to a severe traumatic brain injury he'd had at six weeks. Speech pathology assessments later revealed a 12–18 month delay in his language skills, including both auditory comprehension and expressive communication. Julian was diagnosed with a very significant receptive and expressive language disorder.

If language is liquid, instead of being a sponge, my son was watertight. Something was clogged and plugged. He began regular appointments with a speech pathologist. We needed to break the membrane, burst whatever barrier had stopped his words from flowing. My son didn't share our family word-sense. Because of his injury, Julian's brain had to rewire itself to learn language. As much as he listened, language's music was hard for him to hear.

After my son's language disorder diagnosis, everything felt, looked, sounded, tasted and smelled different to me. Language was how I'd found order in the world, but what gave me structure and meaning was disordered and confusing for Julian. Words were only a tiny fraction of the universe; my senses had to readapt for him. There were other languages to master beyond language – tactile, visual, vocal – and I needed to completely rethink my word-oriented perception of the world to communicate, bond and connect with my son.

Despite early intervention speech therapy, Julian's language abilities at nearly four years old were equivalent to those of a two-year-old. While he better understood English when he listened, his speech still wasn't clear. Similar to my limited Tagalog skills, my son's brain injury meant that he had difficulty learning the other half of the song. So, like anyone who doesn't know the lyrics but still wants to sing along, Julian ad-libbed. He used his imagination and just made up the words.

Julian invented his own private language: 'Julianish'. He developed its unique vocabulary, crafted its distinct grammar and syntax – all built from phonemes his mouth could make and structures his brain could climb. Language acquisition flipped. My son had created his own mother tongue, then taught me – his mother – how to speak it.

Outside our family, very few people understood this made-up language so I often needed to translate everything Julian said. I wasn't just my son's interpreter: I literally became his voice. The conduit for his words. For a long time, I was the channel that joined two seas – 'Julianish' and English. What eventually burst the barrier, what finally unblocked my son's words and made them flow, sprang from an unexpected source. It was learning a second language: French.

I decided to try to learn my mother's mother tongue as an adult. Something about Tagalog has always been strangely intuitive to me. I feel a sense for how it works inside my bones. Tagalog is an agglutinative language; English is not. Agglutination is the process of adding affixes to the base of a word, so many complex words in Tagalog are comprised of a root plus various affixes on either side. Roots stay the same, but the affixes change depending on what role the word plays in the sentence.

This is why Tagalog and other agglutinative languages – like Finnish, Turkish and Hungarian – can have extremely long words. One of the longest words in Tagalog is the 32-letter, 14-syllable *pinakanakapagpapabagabag-damdamin*. It means 'the most emotionally upsetting thing' and is built from two root words – *bagabag* and *damdamin* – with multiple affixes added on both sides. My mum likes to tell this story about Filipinos in an elevator to explain how agglutination in Tagalog works:

A Filipino man is in an elevator, on his way down to the ground floor. At the fourth floor, the elevator stops. The doors open, and a Filipino woman walks in.

'*Bababa ba?*' she asks.

'*Bababa,*' he replies.

That root word *baba* means 'go down'. In Tagalog, you repeat the first syllable to change a verb to future form, so *ba* plus *baba* translates to 'going down'. Add the enclitic particle *ba* to the end of any noun, pronoun, verb, adverb or adjective and you change it into a question. So *bababa ba* ('going down?') and *bababa* ('going down') is an entire conversation you can have in Tagalog using only one syllable.

Now let's keep agglutinating. To change the root word *baba* ('go down') again, add the affix *ma* (to make it an adjective) and you get *mababa* ('low'). Add *pa* (to express manner) and you get *pababa* ('downward'). Add *ka-an* (to express quality of being something) and you have *kababaan* ('lowland'). Add *an* (to express action to an object) and you get *babaan* ('take something downstairs'), but add a different affix *an* (to change the object) and you get *babaan* ('reduce something in size, value, or difficulty'), but then add another *an* (to express a location) and you get *babaan* ('the landing place for a vehicle').

Tagalog grammar is complicated and subtle. For native English speakers, agglutination is counterintuitive, but for some reason I understand it instinctively. I've listened to it since birth. Turns out Tagalog lurks in my unconscious mind.

A recent study examining the unconscious influence of early language development in the brain showed that Chinese children adopted by French-speaking Canadian families as babies still retained a dormant knowledge of their original mother tongue, Mandarin. When listening to spoken Mandarin, the adoptees displayed the same brain activity as native Chinese speakers. Despite not being able to understand or speak the language, Mandarin sounds still lit up areas of the adoptees' brains associated with language processing. On the other hand, children who'd never heard Mandarin didn't associate its sounds with language at all. Neurocognitive traces of Mandarin were written into the adoptees' brains, even though they'd left China when they were infants. Inside the brain, mother tongue sticks around.

This explained why whenever I listened to Tagalog, I involuntarily followed a lot of it. Deep inside my brain, my neurons knew its sounds were language. But how come when I opened my mouth to speak Tagalog, I was inarticulate?

Language is mapped all over the human brain but it lies predominantly in two places: Wernicke's area, concerned with the comprehension of language; and Broca's area, concerned with the production of speech (although this region also plays a role in language comprehension). Second languages are stored differently in Broca's area depending on when we learn them. Children who learn to speak more than one language simultaneously have one uniform primary Broca's area – so inside my mother's brain, English and Tagalog are entangled in the same place.

People who learn a second language in adolescence or adulthood possess spatially separate Broca's areas, one for each language. After reaching a certain age, our primary Broca's area becomes hardwired to speak our mother tongue (or tongues). Once cells in this region are tuned to one or more native languages, eventually they're fixed. While Tagalog was encoded into my Wernicke's area (concerned with comprehension) when I was an infant, and my brain can intuitively understand it, I didn't speak it early enough. My primary Broca's area is now entirely dedicated to speaking English. Each extra language I learn will create an ancillary Broca's region of its own.

Neural hardwiring to our native language even occurs in our brainstem – our reptilian brain, responsible for our basic vital life functions – which is why speaking our mother tongue feels as automatic as breathing. When we speak our first language, we don't need to carefully think about how to pronounce a word, conjugate a verb or construct a sentence. Knowing our mother tongue's sounds, systems and structure is instinctive, like a reflex. Speaking a second language learned as an adult isn't reflexive; it's more like hunting or foraging – or recalling a memory.

Since the Broca's area is concerned with speaking, for adult learners of second languages understanding foreign words isn't always the biggest challenge. Difficulties arise with the motor skills required to form those new words with our mouths, lips and tongues. All of us are born able to make any sound, but at some point in our linguistic development we lose this ability – and before that, we lose our ability to hear certain sounds.

My mouth, like my brain, is hardwired to speak Australian English. I'll never have complete native fluency in Tagalog because my lips aren't physically able to produce all the right noises. So I'm passive bilingual: able to comprehend Tagalog, not able to master speaking it. I can't untie my tongue to speak my mother's mother tongue fluently. When I speak any language, no matter how hard I try to retrain my mouth, I can't shake my hard Australian vowels. This is also why I speak French with an Australian accent.

In French, the word for language and tongue is the same – *la langue* – so the French language is also the French tongue: *la langue française*. I studied French at school for six years, from the age of twelve, but didn't start early enough to sound like a native speaker. My French is much better than my Tagalog, though; I've spent more time practising its grammar and building my vocabulary.

Even then, my passive understanding of French is much better than my active spoken French. I can watch a French film without subtitles, or read a French newspaper or novel without a dictionary, and I'll understand almost every word. I can even write reasonably well in French – definitely not poetry, but I can churn out pretty good formal letters to schoolteachers, angry emails to internet service providers and text messages to friends.

When I speak French, it's a different story. My tongue gets tied. I've lived in France so I can speak French fine, but it doesn't feel automatic. Part of me falls away, like the language itself severs a piece of my personality. I don't sound like myself when I'm speaking French; I have an alter ego. My husband even has a name for my French-speaking secret identity. We call her Antoinette.

Antoinette says *oui* too much, even when she doesn't mean it. She nods more than she should, and she laughs when things aren't funny. But Antoinette isn't funny herself: she can't tell or get a joke so she has zero sense of humour. Sometimes Antoinette is too polite when she doesn't need to be; other times, she's rude when she should be polite. She's extremely literal and boring, yet always skittish and on edge, and she's highly susceptible to blushing. Most of all, Antoinette gets flustered easily, so whenever she opens her mouth she gets nervous – so often picks the wrong word. *Je déteste Antoinette.*

My mum loves this story:

Paris, 2007. I was twenty-five years old. While taking something hot out of the oven, the top of my finger brushed against the grill and – *voila!* Antonia *brûlée*. Worried my burnt finger would get infected, I strolled the very short distance to the pharmacy on the corner of my street (in Paris, there's one on every corner). At this point, I'd lived in France for almost a year and my French was passable. Generally I got by day-to-day without drawing too many blanks, but there were occasions when I'd have total vocabulary amnesia. My conversation with the pharmacist went something like this (*en français*):

Antonia: 'Bonjour, Madame!'

Madame La Pharmacienne: 'Bonjour, Mademoiselle, how can I help you today?'

Antonia: 'I think I need a cream or ointment. I have ... erm ... *[searching brain for the French word for burn]* a *flamant* on my finger. What would you recommend?'

Madame: 'Excusez-moi?'

Antonia: 'For a *flamant*. On my finger.'

Madame La Pharmacienne's face changed from puzzled to bright red with laughter. She called to everyone else in the store, who rushed over to the counter, and made me repeat it again. Upon hearing what I'd just said, everyone in the pharmacy turned bright red with laughter themselves. The French really seemed to love pointing and laughing at people; I wondered if there was an ointment to apply for mass hysteria. I was turning bright red for a different reason altogether.

'*Pardon*, Madame,' I whispered. 'What exactly did I say?'

'*Flamant*! Like this!'

The woman stood on one foot and bent her other at a right angle, exactly like ... A flamingo. I had just told everyone that I had a flamingo on my finger. Unfortunately for me, there was no ointment to fix my flamingo – or my embarrassment – but the pharmacist did give me a lovely topical cream for my burn. I never went back to that particular pharmacy. But just so you don't make the same mistake I did, the word for burn in French is *brûlure*.

We moved to Paris in 2006, when Julian was four years old. He didn't speak a single word of French but, then again, he didn't exactly speak English either. Without any means to communicate with his teacher or classmates, I was nervous about sending him to a French school. On the night before his first day at *l'école maternelle* (preschool in France), I taught Julian how to say one thing in French: that he needed to go to the bathroom, please. That phrase, I figured, was more essential than hello or goodbye, or how to introduce himself. Plus it'd save him future embarrassment. This I knew from personal experience: I had an accident on my first day of kindy because I was too shy to ask my teacher where to find the bathroom.

L'école maternelle wasn't an easy transition for Julian. We'd moved to a new country so he was overwhelmed by countless cultural differences: the food (no Vegemite sandwiches: his school served foie gras to four-year-olds every Wednesday); the school uniform (the children wore smocks with white Peter Pan collars, just like the little girls from *Madeline* – black for boys, pink for girls); the etiquette (there's a reason we use that French word in English); and, of course, the new language.

For the first few weeks, Julian was completely silent at preschool. He cried when I dropped him off and I'd wave goodbye nearly in tears myself, worried we'd made a huge mistake coming to Paris. Why had I thought moving to France would be a good idea? Julian already had developmental problems; I was terrified that living in Paris was just going to make his life more problematic.

Julian proved this anxiety wrong. Within a few months of total immersion, my son spoke French fluently, with a perfect Parisian accent. And his spoken English was suddenly clearer too. The more French he learned, the better his English sounded. Somehow, living in France ended up completely unlocking the enigma of language in his brain.

Since Julian started speaking French at the age of four, his brain is now hardwired to speak English and French; the two languages are stored in one uniform Broca's area. Neurons for both languages live and fire together in the same spot of tissue – and they always will. Our brains have two types of visible tissue: grey matter and white matter. Grey matter makes up the bulk of nerve cells in the brain, and grey matter density has been linked to language, memory and intelligence. Brain imaging comparing the brains of multilingual and monolingual people has showed that bilingual brains have denser grey matter in their Broca's areas. As Julian acquired more French, his English improved – the second language increased his Broca's area grey matter density and, subsequently, his abilities accelerated across his first language too.

Beyond language, evidence from a number of studies suggests that being bilingual enhances the brain's executive function – planning, problem solving, memory – and kids with acquired brain injury often struggle with executive functioning. Not long after moving to Paris, Julian's memory improved and the developmental gap between him and his peers started to close. Becoming bilingual literally changed the structure of Julian's brain and helped him overcome his language disorders, and his brain injury. Ten years later, you'd never know he ever had them.

We lived in Paris for four years, until Julian was eight. Over that time, French became Julian's dominant language. He spoke it all day at school and with his friends. We heard French everywhere – on the bus, at the supermarket, at the park. He played with his Lego in French, he watched French television and movies, he dreamed in French. Julian even started speaking English with a French accent, saying things like stormtroop-*eur*, and stressing the last syllable on every word.

At his school in Paris, they taught the children a second language – English – but Julian didn't immediately realise the language they'd learned in English class was the same language we spoke at home.

'What does this say?' Julian pointed at his homework. 'In English.'

'This is the Eiffel Tower,' I said, reading from the worksheet.

'No, silly,' he said, laughing. 'That's not how you say it in English. You say: *Zis iz zee Eiffel Tower*! That's how the English teacher says it.'

'With a French accent! We speak English with each other, you know. We're speaking English right now.'

'We are?'

I nodded. 'Which language did you think we spoke together?'

Julian shrugged. 'I dunno. Australian?'

In France, French wasn't a foreign language. We were the foreigners; English was just another foreign language there. As someone who'd grown up speaking English in a predominantly English-speaking culture, this was an important jolt of perspective: to live in a country where I was an immigrant who spoke a second language at home; to be the foreign parent of a child who'd eventually speak our adopted language better than I did.

Always being able to effortlessly express myself, to be articulate and communicate without obstacles, was an invisible privilege I'd taken for granted as an English speaker living in Australia. Language barriers can alienate, marginalise; without mastering the native tongue, can we ever truly penetrate and understand another country? Do we filter other cultures through the alien fabric of our own? My awkward spoken French made me lose part of my identity, but living in France automatically assigned me a new one anyway – an outsider. Foreigner and stranger are the same word in French: *l'étranger*.

Mother tongue suddenly became more important to me as a foreigner, and as a mother. As Julian assimilated into a new culture, I worried about his first language getting swallowed up by French. In Paris, our family was his only steady source of English, so I felt an obligation to ensure my son kept speaking, improving and developing his English language skills. Language is liquid, but undertows still swell below surface currents. We'd read more English books, watch more English movies – swim against the tide.

When Julian was six, his teacher suggested that I stop teaching him how to read in English at home. Julian needed to focus on reading in only French, she'd said. Learning to read both languages at once confused Julian, and the teacher stressed that his literacy in French was much more important than English literacy. In the moment, I bristled at this suggestion – how dare this teacher advocate one language over another, over mine – but on reflection, I wonder how much my irritation was bounded by an inheritance of imperial thinking of my own.

Colonisation is deeply imprinted in Australian history and culture, as a British colony yoked to the British Empire. Within this legacy hide dangerous ideologies: that one society is superior; that one race is inferior; that one group represents civilisation and the other is uncivilised, primitive; that one language is more important than another language; that culture should be homogenised – or dissolved. Australia can't erase its colonial past, and this past carries an implicit message that erasure and cultural supremacy are okay.

France has a long imperial history of its own, dating back to their colonisation of the Americas in the early 16th century. Napoleon Bonaparte declared himself Emperor of France and expanded the French overseas territories to Asia and Africa; his nephew, Napoleon III, doubled the Empire's area during his reign. And France sees itself as an inclusive nation with universal values.

So when Julian's teacher expected us to prioritise French, it wasn't an unreasonable demand in her mind. Julian lived in France; he must read French. Was this different from Australians who expect children of immigrants to prioritise learning to read in English over their mother tongue?

Liberté, égalité, fraternité – the French national motto insists on freedom, equality and unity, but it doesn't seem universal. There's no freedom to wear a hijab in French public schools; it's illegal. Income inequality is highly visible in Paris: it's one of the most expensive cities in the world, yet also home to nearly thirty thousand homeless people. Until the mid-1980s, French immigration policy demanded that all immigrants abandon their cultures and traditions – to live in France you needed to become French. You must assimilate.

Under the republican model of integration, all French citizens are the same; in theory, the state doesn't see colour, race and religion. But in practice, I didn't think Paris felt culturally inclusive or socially cohesive. Instead of embracing diversity, the interminable idea of a French identity had created an opposing identity of otherness. Ideologically, France wanted a homogeneous society, but that meant any trace of cultural diversity would vanish; it was just cultural supremacy by another name. Discrimination and racial tension still persisted in what was supposed to be an egalitarian society, built on a foundation of unity.

I understood why real integration wasn't happening. I felt fiercely resistant to total assimilation because that would be giving up who I was. But even if I'd left my Australian identity at the border when I'd entered France, I'd still always be seen as a foreigner in Paris, an other – never French. Besides, French culture and language weren't superior to my culture and language; I didn't want mine erased. At home, I continued championing English so Julian wouldn't lose it. But I started to question my thinking about culture, asking myself what fuelled this stubborn preservation instinct.

In our neighbourhood in Paris, it was often accepted that some American expats could only speak English, but anyone heard speaking Arabic was usually cajoled to speak French. This selective discrimination made me uneasy, but it also reminded me of similar attitudes in Australia – how I'd often heard other kids yell 'You're in Australia, speak Australian!' to the Chinese and Korean students at my school, but rarely to the European kids. Besides, the English language wasn't really Australian; it wasn't native to the land. How many Indigenous languages have been lost since 1788? In France, the general attitude was that speaking French was paramount, but their preservation instinct at least made some sense: the French are indigenous to France. In Australia,

English reigned supreme but it was an imperial language, not native: it'd been imposed.

Language was legacy to me, but the more I wondered why, the more it looked like we treat some legacies as more important than others. Had I inherited some colonial impulse from my British ancestors, some unspoken conviction of my own cultural supremacy? This was actually language as power play, heritage as hierarchy. Did protecting my first language feel especially crucial to me because it was English – the mother tongue of the motherland?

That intense urge to sustain my son's mother tongue in Paris, to safeguard our common language, often made me think about my own mother and Tagalog. Why didn't my mum feel like she needed to preserve her mother tongue with me?

When I was seven years old, my mum and I visited my grandmother in Manila. This was the first time I'd been to the Philippines since I was a baby and I didn't remember that earlier trip. I spent my seventh birthday aboard the plane from Sydney. During the flight, Qantas stewards brought a small chocolate cake to my seat and all of economy class sang 'Happy Birthday' across the rows and aisles.

My grandmother had already planned my birthday in Manila; she'd organised a big party on the day after we arrived. 'All your family and friends will be there,' Ona told me. 'I've sent invitations to everyone. You'll have so much fun.' But my family was in Burwood and all my friends were in the Blue Mountains; I wasn't sure how they'd get to my party – or who else my grandmother had invited.

In the Philippines, it's tradition for a child's seventh birthday to be a huge celebration. I'm still not sure why; I've asked family and searched the internet for some historical or cultural reason but all I've found out is precisely what my relatives told me: just because. Filipinos love parties, they'll find any excuse to celebrate, and these parties generally revolve around food.

My seventh birthday party was held in the function room of a hotel in Metro Manila. When I walked in, the first thing I noticed was the vast cornucopia of food: a figurine-covered *Snow White and the Seven Dwarfs* cake from Goldilocks Bakery, a fairy-floss machine, dozens of jugs of *buko* juice, and a sprawling buffet – steel tray after steel tray filled with *bistek, pancit, pinakbet, lumpia, leche flan*.

The second thing I noticed was that the room was full of strangers. Loud strangers. Loud strangers who all spoke really fast, yelling in a language that I didn't speak. And since I was the birthday girl, everyone was yelling and smiling at me. I tried to hide behind my mother's dress but I wasn't invisible; a swarm of excited Filipino relatives had already started rushing towards us.

'*Ganda-ganda naman ni Tonia!*' a woman, who was probably my aunt or second cousin twice removed, shrieked. She squeezed my cheeks and gave me a firm hug. I could taste her hairspray in my mouth as she squashed my face into a satin shoulder pad (it was 1989). '*Ang* tall *mo! Tsaka maputi.*'

I smiled and nodded, before quickly turning to my mother. 'What did she say, Mummy?' I whispered.

'That you're tall and pale.'

'Oh,' I said, pulling at the hem of my pink party dress and feeling like a circus freak. I turned back to the shoulder-padded woman. 'Thank you,' I replied politely, although what she'd said sounded more like an insult than a compliment to me.

'Tonia, you don't know how to talk in Tagalog?' my aunt/second cousin twice removed asked.

I shook my head and blushed. I remember feeling a sense of inadequacy that I couldn't speak Tagalog. On the way to Manila, we'd stopped over in Hong Kong, and I hadn't understood the airport announcements and couldn't read the Chinese characters on the signs. That seemed different; not understanding Cantonese hadn't feel like a personal shortcoming. But I was half-Filipino; why didn't I know my family's language? Speaking Tagalog felt like something I *should* be able to do – like a responsibility I'd rejected instead of embraced. I spent the rest of my seventh birthday party feeling embarrassed about it, and confused.

Later that evening, after the party had ended and all the guests had left, I asked my mum why I couldn't speak Tagalog. How come she'd never taught me? Mum told me that Tagalog wasn't a very useful language. Since I was only seven years old, I took her word for it. Before then, I'd never thought of languages as functional. I hadn't realised that they could be useful – or not – or that one language was more practical to speak than another. But I wasn't entirely convinced: surely being able to communicate with my Filipino family was useful too.

Twenty-seven years later, I've come to realise that my mother's attitude towards Tagalog back then wasn't just about being pragmatic. It concerned her identity. Mum's preference for speaking English herself, and with me, wasn't prioritising the usefulness of a language. This was a declaration of *who* she wanted to be.

Her dismissal of the importance of Tagalog, of her mother tongue, was a reflection of my mum's personal reinvention – as an English speaker. This reincarnation started early. Although English is one of the official languages of the Philippines and my mum grew up speaking it as well as Tagalog, Filipino English has its own distinct diction and pronunciation. As well as some of its own formulations like 'go ahead' for 'I'll leave now' and 'eat-all-you-can' for 'buffet', Filipino English also has slight variations from standard Western English syntax – most notably, the placement of 'already' in awkward spots.

Phonologically, the sounds of Filipino English closely resemble American English, and since the letters *c, f, j, q, v, x* and *z* don't exist in traditional Tagalog, many Filipinos confuse *p* and *f* and substitute *b* for *v* (*bery good!*). Listen to my mother speak English and you'll hear an Australian accent, with deliberate and elegantly modulated Oxford elocution. Her voice doesn't broadcast her origins: you'd never know she lived in the Philippines until she was eleven years old.

Much is revealed about us by the way we speak. Accent is cultural imprint: it betrays our history and geography. Right now I live in the United States, so whenever I open my mouth and speak English with an Australian accent, people immediately want to identify where I'm from – my voice tells them something about who I am. In Sydney, I didn't sound foreign, but the way I speak is a marker of difference here. Whether I like it or not, my accent makes me stand out. It instantly labels me as different. In

San Francisco, Australian accents are definitely the exception to the rule.

Since accent and language are associated with nationality, we can't pretend they're not linked to ideas about race. Amy Tan wrote an essay about the English she spoke with her Chinese mother – that her mother's 'broken' English was her mother tongue – and she discussed the problematic ways we treat immigrants who don't speak their adopted language fluently: 'I've been giving more thought to the kind of English my mother speaks. Like others, I have described it to people as "broken" or "fractured" English. But I wince when I say that. It has always bothered me that I can think of no way to describe it other than "broken", as if it were damaged and needed to be fixed, as if it lacked a certain wholeness and soundness. I've heard other terms used, "limited English", for example. But they seem just as bad, as if everything is limited, including people's perceptions of the limited English speaker. I know this for a fact, because when I was growing up, my mother's "limited" English limited my perception of her. I was ashamed of her English. I believed that her English reflected the quality of what she had to say. That is, because she expressed them imperfectly her thoughts were imperfect. And I had plenty of empirical evidence to support me: the fact that people in department stores, at banks, and at restaurants did not take her seriously, did not give her good service, pretended not to understand her, or even acted as if they did not hear her.'

Language isn't only connected to race; it also relates to class. Like Amy Tan, Ian McEwan wrote an essay about the language he inherited from his mother, except it wasn't a foreign language. McEwan's mother was extremely self-conscious about her accent, with its double negatives and mismatched plurals, and would modulate her voice so it wouldn't reveal she'd been brought up in poverty and had a childhood speech impediment: 'I don't write like my mother, but for many years I spoke like her, and her particular, timorous relationship with language has shaped my own. There are people who move confidently within their own horizons of speech; whether it is Cockney, Estuary, RP or Valley Girl, they stride with the unselfconscious ease of a landowner on his own turf. My mother was never like that. She never owned the language she spoke. Her displacement within the intricacies of English class, and the uncertainty that went with it, taught her to regard language as something that might go off in her face, like a letter bomb. A word bomb.'

In a lecture delivered at New York Public Library, Zadie Smith spoke of how the voice she speaks with now is not the voice of her childhood; it was a voice she picked up at university, but it's now become her only voice. 'My own childhood had been the story of this and that combined, of the synthesis of disparate things. It never occurred to me that I was leaving the London district of Willesden for Cambridge. I thought I was adding Cambridge to Willesden, this new way of talking to that old way. Adding a new kind of knowledge to a different kind I already had. And for a while, that's how it was: at home, during the holidays, I spoke with my old voice, and in the old voice seemed to feel and speak things that I couldn't express in college, and vice versa. I felt a sort of wonder at the flexibility of the thing. Like being alive twice. But flexibility is something that requires work if it is to be maintained. Recently my double voice has deserted me for a single one, reflecting the smaller world into which my work has led me. Willesden was a big, colourful, working-class sea; Cambridge was a smaller, posher pond, and almost univocal; the literary world is a puddle. This voice I picked up along the way is no longer an exotic garment I put on like a college gown whenever I choose – now it is my only voice, whether I want it or not. I regret it; I should have kept both voices alive in my mouth. They were both a part of me. But how the culture warns against it!'

Smith then speaks about George Bernard Shaw's play *Pygmalion* and Eliza Doolittle's identity crisis: of how Eliza changed her voice but then lost who she was. One of my favourite childhood films was *My Fair Lady*. I loved the sets and costumes, but mostly I loved the songs; I still know all the lyrics to 'Wouldn't It Be Loverly', sung in the strong Cockney accent of Audrey Hepburn's Eliza Doolittle. After embarking on speech training with Henry Higgins, Eliza figures out how to speak with an upper-class English accent – but when she returns to her old life, Eliza no longer fits in.

We are our voices; our voices are who we are. My husband's Romanian grandfather used to say that 'you are as many people as languages you speak' (he spoke seven languages, so was seven people), but I think that applies to how we speak too. Each language and each accent adds another layer of identity. If one is lost, we lose something of ourselves.

I now see some of Eliza Doolittle in my mother, in how when she modified her voice, her identity transformed. I imagine my mum at eleven years old, suddenly finding herself at boarding school in a new country, desperately wanting to blend in with the rest of the girls in her class. This was Sydney in the early 1970s; the other kids would've seen my mother's long dark hair and Asian features as different. So Mum assimilated as best she could. She couldn't change her face, but she could change her voice. Sound Australian, act Australian, and shed her Filipino skin. Just like Eliza Doolittle: by changing the way she spoke, my mother changed the way she'd be treated by others, how she was seen, and, ultimately, who she was.

Her birthplace sheds light on *why* my mum was so willing to reinvent herself. Like Australia, the Philippines has its own long colonial history. In 1521, Portuguese explorer Ferdinand Magellan claimed the islands that he'd discovered in the Pacific for the Spanish King. For 333 years, the Philippines was a Spanish colony. A Filipino nationalist movement eventually led to the Philippine Revolution against Spanish colonial rule in 1896, but although the Philippines declared independence from Spain in 1898, Spain was at war with the United States of America. After Spain's defeat in the Spanish–American War, the Philippines became a colony of the United States in 1901. It wasn't until 1946 – after the Japanese occupation – that the Philippines gained full sovereignty and became an independent republic.

Four centuries of colonial rule – and the cultural imperialism that comes with it – have left a deep imprint on Filipino culture and national identity. Between the 16th and 19th centuries, the Philippines had a colonial caste system, basically an ethnic social hierarchy imposed by the Spanish. This system of racial stratification of Filipino society was used for taxation: *Negritos* (indigenous Aeta Filipinos) and *Indios* (indigenous Austronesian Filipinos) paid a base tax rate; *Sangleys* (Chinese) paid quadruple the base rate; *Insulares* (those with full Spanish ancestry) and *Peninsulares* (born in Spain) paid no tax. The darker your skin, the less power you had. The caste system wasn't abolished until the Philippine Declaration of Independence from Spain in 1898 – around the time my great-grandparents were born.

How do you disentangle 300 years of that racial hierarchy – which explicitly created a division of superior and inferior ethnicities – from the Filipino social consciousness, even today? My great-grandparents were heirs to a fragile national identity; their parents lived within that caste system. Emeterio Barcelon y Barcelo-Soriano, my mother's paternal grandfather, was born in 1897 – in the middle of a revolution. He was a writer and an academic, lectured in Spanish at universities in Manila, and wrote hymns and books in Spanish. My great-grandfather was, apparently, the closest thing to a poet laureate the American Philippines ever had. He encouraged my mother's Spanish when she was a child. She learnt, by heart, at his knees, José Rizal's *Mi última adiós* – written just before Rizal's execution at the hands of a firing squad in the fortified precinct of their walled city, the colonial core of Spanish Manila, *Intramuros*.

My great-grandfather's love of the Spanish language, and immense pride in his Spanish heritage, was amplified by the dark legacies of colonialism, by all the messages of cultural supremacy and inferiority he'd internalised. His eldest son, José Maria Barcelon, my grandfather, inherited that legacy of this cultural baggage – its complex burden cast shadows on his identity. My mother was born into the shadows of these legacies; she is heir to a fragile yet rich national identity too.

So I understand why my mother didn't teach me Tagalog. She comes from a country occupied by the Spanish and then the Americans for four centuries, which delineated power and importance by ethnicity only two generations before she was born. Hard-wired sentiments and beliefs about class and race – like having darker skin lowers one's status, or native dialects are less important than English – permeated her family, their thinking, and the way they spoke and behaved, even if they weren't conscious of it. My mother was willing to abandon her Filipino heritage because Filipino culture told her it didn't have much value.

Often subconscious but sometimes overt, these beliefs still persist all over the Philippines today. But it's not that difficult for me to understand how a population of over 90 million people have an internalised inferiority complex: Australia has its own history of cultural cringe. Inadequacy, doubt, uncertainty: these are the by-products of colonialism. Cultural baggage is psychologically complex; it can be so pervasive it becomes invisible, and we don't even realise that we're carrying generations of these heavy loads on our backs.

In Australia, I'm always asked where I'm from – because of how I look. Although my fifth great-grandfather arrived in 1788 on the First Fleet, although I'm a seventh-generation Australian, I don't look Caucasian, so I must not be from Australia. I grew up in a liminal space: half white, half dominant culture; half Asian, half minority. Both, but also neither; being a hybrid excludes me from being white, and from being Asian. In my extended white Australian family, I'm the Asian one, but in my extended Filipino family, I'm white.

In the Philippines, there's a word for people like me. I am a *mestiza* – mixed. Back in colonial times, *mestizos* were anybody of mixed heritage, but today the word is used for those who are part white. When my Filipino relatives shriek about how pale I am, to my ears it sounds like they think I'm pasty and gross, but they're not actually insulting me. Being pale in the Philippines is good. Beauty standards in the Philippines are still steeped in colonial mentality. The Filipino beauty industry is built around the belief that white is beautiful – which sends the dangerous message that, therefore, brown is not.

An investigative journalism study found that 50 per cent of women in the country use whitening products on their skin: whitening soaps, whitening creams, whitening pills, whitening injections. Most Filipino celebrities and models are *mestizos* or *mestizas,* so its mixed faces like mine you'll primarily see on billboards, in ads, on TV, in the cinema. These images constantly reinforce the stigma against brown skin, even though they don't accurately reflect the majority of the Philippines: *mestizos* and *mestizas* make up less than 4 per cent of the Filipino population. By positioning mixed-heritage Filipinos at the centre of their culture, most Filipinos are placed at the periphery.

So it's only natural that the Philippines' complicated history, of 400 years of colonialism, of still being bombarded by the idea that white is beautiful in the media, would also affect Filipino attitudes about native languages. As recently as 2011, students in schools across the country were being penalised – sometimes even punished – for speaking their mother tongue instead of English at school. Just like pale skin and Western features are markers of beauty, English is the language of success.

For Filipino children, this idea is damaging on both psychological and cultural levels. Since language and mother tongue are entwined with identity, being punished for speaking your native dialect is essentially punishment for being yourself. And when young children are conditioned to associate speaking English with success, eventually they'll believe their native language to be irrelevant. When they grow up and one day have children of their own, they won't think it's worth passing their native language on to the next generation.

Exactly like my mother.

She is one among many others who've done the same.

As if language were a numbers game, I imagine my mum thought not passing Tagalog down to me was no great loss. That whatever I'd gain from speaking it wouldn't be worth the time she'd need to invest in teaching Tagalog to me. After unravelling the dark legacies and shadows of both my Filipino and Australian background, I can make sense of how she came to this conclusion; I get it. My mum wasn't driven by some desire for wanton cultural annihilation. But until I tried to learn Tagalog myself as an adult, I had this unshakeable feeling like I'd been robbed of something important, like what had been lost in the linguistic fire was a piece of my mum.

When I was a teenager and fought with my mother – in English – it was me who stormed out of the room with tears in my eyes. She was the one who didn't understand, not me. We were foreign to each other, strangers. Our miscommunication must have stemmed from misunderstanding. I believed that my mum was behind some wall, a veneer, hiding inside this second language that she'd mastered, studied at Oxford, spoke with erudition and formality. Nothing about the way my mum speaks English is raw, not like the way she speaks Tagalog. When I was younger, I thought understanding Tagalog would make me understand my mother better, would help me figure out the raw emotions I suspected she tried to disguise. I wished I knew her mother tongue because I longed to really know my mother.

Now that I'm older – and a mother myself – I realise it was never that straightforward. Tagalog wasn't a key to unlock every mystery about my mum. In fact, the more Tagalog I learned, the less I believed there was ever a key. We're all archipelagos, made up of thousands of islands; some of these islands are too remote to reach. There are parts of all of us that are simply unknowable, places that other people will never completely understand. Miscommunication and misunderstanding don't only spring from linguistic and cultural differences. They happen in every language, even when people speak the same one and use the same words; they happen because we're all different human beings.

My mother never taught me her mother tongue. Part of my mother tongue is its absence. But I'm the basin where two bodies of water meet; I am the watershed where two mouths of different ancient rivers converge. I'm shaped by the undercurrents of two languages, English and Tagalog: the mother tongues of both my parents. So I'm not the trench where these currents stop flowing.

I am a source myself.

A confluence, a conduit, a channel, not a dam. I am my son's mother, and his mother tongue. The family I come from speaks several languages, but the family I made has created its own.

We are all fluent in the private languages of our families. Not just in the shared verbal languages we speak, but also in the ways that we learn to communicate and miscommunicate with each other, how we understand and misunderstand the people we love. We might become fluent in what's said between the words, in the silences, when we stop to breathe.

We may not ever hear what's in the void. Sometimes we need to translate and interpret each other, or define and redefine ourselves, or find new meanings beyond the reaches of our vocabularies. Each generation creates its own language, where mother tongues mix and merge and cascade down to the next length of our rivers, because language is liquid. Fluid. Mother tongue is the ever-flowing stream that shapes and reshapes our families, our identities, our brains, our cultures, our histories and our futures. Language is the source from where all our stories spring.

Super Special #1

Jonathan Franzen said, 'The first thing reading teaches us is how to be alone,' but I think that's a misanthrope's pearl of wisdom. Books taught me the opposite lesson: that I'd always have friends, even if they were imaginary. I'll never forget the first book I chose for myself – a real one, not a picture book, a bound paperback novel with chapters. I was seven. It was 1989: the year students protested in Tiananmen Square, earthquakes hit San Francisco and Newcastle, everyone had *Teenage Mutant Ninja Turtles* fever, and, more than 15 000km away from where I was, Taylor Swift was born. My monumental moment of 1989 took place in the kids' section of Megalong Books in Leura, where I was about to meet Kristy, Mary Anne, Claudia, Stacey, Dawn, and Mallory for the first time. How to be alone? Franzen obviously never read The Baby-sitters Club.

(Imagine if he had; Kristy would've quickly knocked that thinly disguised contempt for women right out of him.)

It was one of those exhilaration-filled first days of the school holidays. Mum took me into town and said she'd buy me a new book (I think she was less exhilarated about the holidays). Book-choosing was a responsibility I took very seriously, and I carefully scanned the shelves in the bookshop. Alison Lester? Outgrown her. The Berenstain Bears? Talking animals were too juvenile for mature seven-year-old me. Recently I'd started reading Roald Dahl, but even his books had pictures. Nope; sorry, Quentin Blake. I'd just reached the age of reason; what I needed was a big book for big kids.

A row of gelati-coloured spines caught my eye. All of these books were written by the same author: Ann M. Martin. They had compelling, grown-up-sounding titles like *Claudia and the Phantom Phone Calls* (who, or what, was calling her?), and *The Truth About Stacey* (what was it?!) – but I'd never heard of The Baby-sitters Club before. Nobody in my class at my school read them (this was probably because I was at a Steiner school in the Blue Mountains where we mostly did arts and crafts; I'm still an excellent finger knitter). These pink and yellow books were real novels, looked like the kind of serious books my parents read. I chose the thickest one on the shelf because I knew that long books were more difficult to read, and therefore more important. It was *The Baby-sitters Club Super Special #1: Baby-sitters on Board!*

On the cover, some exceedingly friendly-looking American teenage girls with side-ponytails and wide smiles stood on the deck of a cruise ship. Stencilled on lifesaver rings attached to the deck railing were the words *Ocean Princess*. The teenagers wore oversized jumpers with shorts, rolled-down socks with sneakers. 'It's the baby-sitting adventure of a lifetime!' the caption said. Baby-sitting! Adventure! My palms began to sweat. Those two activities were the domains of big kids; this was the sort of big-kid book I should read. Beams of celestial light probably spilled through the window of Megalong Books onto where I was standing; a distant choir probably started singing. It felt like a moment of revelation, like the stylish and happy girls in the cover illustration of *Baby-sitters on Board!* were waving directly at me. I immediately found my mum and announced that I needed this book.

Too psyched to wait until I got home, I cracked the spine and started *Super Special #1* in the car. Not even motion sickness could stop me from setting sail on this baby-sitting adventure of a lifetime. Several pages into the story, I learned that The Baby-sitters Club was literally a club of seven baby-sitters/best friends, who lived in Stoneybrook, Connecticut (I wouldn't figure out how to correctly pronounce that word for nearly another year).

Just like a real club, all the members of The Baby-sitters Club had official positions. Kristy Thomas was President of the BSC (because it was her idea); Mary Anne Spier was Secretary (she had the nicest handwriting); Claudia Kishi was Vice President (they held BSC meetings in her bedroom because she had her own phone), Stacey McGill was Treasurer (maths whiz); Dawn Schafer was Alternate Officer (and from California, and became Treasurer when Stacey moved to New York a few books later); and, in later books in the series, Mallory Pike and Jessi Ramsey were Junior Officers (because they were eleven).

In a nutshell, here's the super-absorbing plot of *Super Special #1*: Mallory's dad wins an all-expenses-paid cruise, only there are eight kids in the Pike family so they ask Mary Anne and Stacey if they'll come to baby-sit, but then Kristy's rich stepfather decides that everyone else should also go on this vacation and buys tickets for all, which is how every member of the BSC ends up on the *Ocean Princess* cruising through the Bahamas (with three bonus days in Disney World, Florida). So much happens on this cruise. Secret admirers! Arguments about cleanliness! Illicit manicures! Lost unicorn-charm bracelets! Unlike most books in the BSC series, *Super Special #1* is told from the alternating viewpoints of everyone, including Kristy's little sister Karen – which is why much of the plot revolves around illicit manicures.

Recently, I came home to Sydney for a brief visit and stayed at my dad's house, where I slept in the childhood bedroom of Claudia, my own little sister. I like to think she's named after Claudia in The Baby-sitters Club. Before she was born, I remember Dad asking me what I thought we should name the new baby. Since I was nine years old and at the peak of my BSC mania, without hesitating I suggested Kristy, Mary Anne, Stacey, Claudia, Dawn, Mallory or Jessi – so I'll happily take credit for naming Claudia Hayes. Claudia was living in Madrid while I was back home, so I was able to snoop around her room in private. Collecting dust on her bookshelf were those familiar but now faded gelati-coloured spines: my hand-me-down collection of Baby-sitters Club books, including the one that started my obsession.

I took if off the shelf and blew dust off the cover, slightly alarmed by how old and dated the book looked. Over the 1989 school holidays, I'd read and reread *Super Special #1* until I almost knew it off by heart. I was even reading it while my parents watched the news one night, showing footage of the fall of the Berlin Wall. Every word in all 131 books in the BSC series (plus Super Specials, plus Mysteries, plus spin offs) can't express how much I loved reading *Super Special #1*. Thanks to that book, I still have an irrational desire to cruise the Bahamas and charge manicures to my cabin and buy a unicorn-charm bracelet at Disney World. *Super Special #1* sparked the voracious reader in me. So, at the age of thirty-two, I decided to read it again.

Unfortunately, I couldn't quite recapture the magic of the summer of 1989 in the autumn of 2015. What seemed romantic to me at seven, in Claudia's stowaway secret admirer who kept following her around the ship and leaving her gifts like pearl earrings, actually felt more like creepy stalker behaviour twenty-five years later. And while I enjoyed the lesbian sexual tension undertones I'd previously missed between Mary Anne and her new sophisticated friend, Alexandra Carmody, Ann M. Martin's passion for adverbs was distracting (she said passionately) and the plot was full of worrying implausibilities (like why weren't any adults concerned about Kristy's bizarre friendship with an old man, and why wasn't anyone bothered by the fact that Dawn's cruise-crush was a latently abusive jerk, and seriously, what was the deal with Stacey's constant diabetes shame?).

But I never really read The Baby-sitters Club books for the plots. I loved them because of the characters. Although most of the characters were kind of clichéd, they felt real to me; they really were my friends. Each member of the BSC was a spectacular late-eighties/early-nineties thirteen-year-old girl Jungian archetype. Everyone in The Baby-sitters Club was different, but that never got in the way of their friendship. Ann M. Martin even gave them all their own handwriting. Tomboy Kristy loved baseball and bossing everyone around; she had the clear and confident handwriting of a leader. Shy and bookish Mary Anne loved crying and her boyfriend, Logan; she had ornate, flowing and neat handwriting (a confession: to this day, I still have Mary Anne handwriting because I literally spent months and months copying it). Dreamy and creative Claudia loved junk food but hated school; her handwriting is arty but full of spelling mistakes. Sophisticated and boy-crazy Stacey loved maths and shopping; I'm not sure why exactly but probably because she was boy-crazy, she dotted her *i*s with hearts. Dawn was an eco-warrior neat-freak who always complained about how the weather was warmer in California; she had the free and easy handwriting of someone who grew up in California. I can't remember Mallory and Jessi's handwriting because I just loved them a little bit less, because they were only eleven.

I didn't have a favourite Baby-sitters Club character – I loved them all almost equally – and I saw aspects of myself in all of them. I was ambitious and full of ideas like Kristy, even copying her and starting my own club at school (I was too young to actually babysit so just created a club for the sake of creating a club; our club held meetings at lunchtime and was called . . . Club Sandwich). But I was also as scatterbrained and messy as Claudia – and just like her I was Asian, so I had almond-shaped eyes. I loved Stacey because she was good at maths like me, and I loved Jessi because I did ballet too. I had the anxious temperament of Mary Anne, but was about as cool as nerdy Mallory. I never really had anything in common with Dawn – except that I now live in California. All these girls were creative and confident entrepreneurs, the kind of young women adults trusted and respected, who also seemed to have great time-management skills. They were feminists. I wanted to be like them.

In 1991, we moved from the Blue Mountains to Sydney. No one at my old school in Leura was as into the Baby-sitters Club as I was, nobody ever wanted to play the Baby-sitters Club board game with me, but that was about the change. At my new school, I finally met the Stacey to my Claudia, the Jessi to my Mallory, the Kristy to my Mary Anne (sorry, Dawn). Her name was Eliza. I loved Eliza because she was passionate like Kristy, but also just as sweet as Mary Anne. She had handwriting like Claudia but was much better at spelling, and, like Stacey and me, she was also good at maths. Both of us did ballet like Jessi and we were both about as cool as Mallory. Naturally, Eliza and I became best friends.

We swapped and borrowed each other's BSC books and carefully planned who'd buy which new release in that month's Scholastic Book Club. Eliza and I played the BSC board game together, which involved telling each other a lot of secrets – it was like an early version of the *New York Times* Modern Love column about the thirty-six questions that lead to falling in love – so we knew everything about one another. We watched the TV show and sang the theme song together. Sometimes, when I went to Eliza's house or she came to mine, we'd just sit beside each other and read.

Inevitably, Eliza and I outgrew the series. All the members of the BSC were stuck in the safe haven of Stoneybrook, where the worst thing to happen to anyone was a dead grandmother. Kristy, Mary Anne, Claudia, Stacey, Dawn, Mallory and Jessi never got older – they were trapped in time – but Eliza and I were growing up. The books started to get boring. And similar to how I'd dismissed the Berenstain Bears at seven, eventually I decided that The Baby-sitters Club was too juvenile for a mature eleven-year-old like me. I packed my collection away for my little sister, Claudia – to save for when she was ready to read them. The last book I read in the series was *#65: Stacey's Big Crush*.

I discovered many years later that Ann M. Martin stopped writing The Baby-sitters Club books herself after #35. Realising half the books I'd loved intensely were ghostwritten felt like a betrayal. On my book tour last year, I was asked in an interview was which author inspired me to become a writer. I said Ian McEwan because he writes the sort of books I'd love to write, is the sort of novelist that I'd one day like to become – but this answer wasn't entirely true. The person who inspired me to become a writer was really Ann M. Martin.

I'd written to Ann M. Martin in 1990, telling her how much I loved the series, and I'm pretty sure I sent at least three ideas for new BSC books – strangely, I don't think she used any of them! I also asked her if she was ever going to come to Australia and if writing books was something people could really do for a job. Several months later, I received a reply.

Enclosed in the envelope was a black-and-white photograph of Ann M. Martin, with a perm and a giant pile of her fan mail. Her letter to me was typed, printed on a dot-matrix printer, with perforated bumps running down the edges of the paper. Ann M. Martin had signed it herself in blue ink, and I instantly recognised her handwriting – it was the same as Mary Anne's, and mine. She thanked me for taking the time to write to her and for the story ideas; said she'd love to come to Australia one day; and that yes, writing books was her full-time job. Her advice to me was this: if I wanted to become a writer when I grew up, I should keep a journal.

Thanks to Ann M. Martin, I've been writing regularly in diaries and journals for the last twenty-six years. I have stacks of them, dozens and dozens. In 2008, I began keeping my journal in Google Docs – all my secrets are on the cloud, in a folder called *Yraid*, just in case hackers or Google employees should ever break into my Drive. I'm sure they wouldn't figure out how to read the word diary backwards.

Last year I went to a book event and saw Sarah Manguso speak in San Francisco about her latest book *Ongoingness*, which is an exploration of her lifelong obsession with writing in her own diary. I'd bought and read the book before the event; Manguso's diary totalled 800 000 words. I didn't know the exact word count of my own Google Docs diary so decided to figure it out. Not including everything I've handwritten in my Mary Anne handwriting, the total was 1.2 million (1.4 million today). When Manguso signed my copy of *Ongoingness,* I told her my crazy diary word count. She gave me a knowing look, like we shared a special secret. *To Antonia,* she wrote on the title page. *1.2 million! Congrats x*

But some of the congratulations should really go to Ann M. Martin.

When Eliza and I were thirteen – the same age as Kristy, Mary Anne, Claudia, Stacey and Dawn – *The Baby-sitters Club: The Movie* was released. It was 1995. We'd long since stopped reading the books; we were Green Day fans now. It was the height of grunge and we lived in band t-shirts. Eliza wore flannel and army pants; I wore miniskirts and Doc Martens boots with knee-high rainbow socks. But we still decided to go see the film together – for old times' sake. In the middle of the movie, I remember Eliza and I shared a look. Maybe we thought we were cooler than Mallory now, but deep down we'd always be members of the BSC.

Thanks to the shining example that Ann M. Martin and the strong friendship bonds in the Baby-sitters Club set for us, Eliza and I are still great friends. Not too long ago, I was over at her house and we were talking about recent books she'd read – including *Freedom* by Jonathan Franzen. It was a shame, Eliza said to me, that you could never quite recapture the magic of childhood reading as an adult. I thought about Franzen's idea that reading first teaches us how to be alone, and remembered quietly reading Baby-sitters Club books beside Eliza on the sofa when we were kids. That was the magic: even when we weren't together on the sofa, we were never alone. We were in Stoneybrook with Kristy, Mary Anne, Claudia, Stacey, Dawn, Mallory and Jessi. What I love most about books is also one of the lyrics in the *Baby-sitters Club* TV show theme song: *you know that your friends are always there.*

A Universe of One's Own

I first read *A Room of One's Own* by Virginia Woolf when I was nineteen years old, during my second year of uni. More accurately, it was read out loud by one of my English lecturers: what originally had been a lecture delivered by Woolf at two women's colleges in Cambridge, delivered more than seventy years later in a lecture theatre at Sydney University. How meta, I'd thought, silently congratulating myself on correctly using the word meta, which I'd learnt in another second-year English lecture. And now here I am, speaking to you about that lecture about a lecture at this Sydney Writers' Festival Curiosity Lecture. The extra meta-ness of this might blow nineteen-year-old Antonia's mind.

Pink highlighter in hand, I enthusiastically underlined paragraph after paragraph of my second-hand copy of *A Room of One's Own,* purchased for $4 from Gleebooks and originally belonging to someone named Janet who wrote her name on the title page. To explore what Woolf calls 'the unsolved problems' of women and fiction, she invents a fictional persona: Mary Seton, a female novelist herself. Why is it, Mary asks, that men have always had power, influence and wealth, while women have had nothing but children? As she dismantles the historical grounds for inequality of creative expression between the sexes, she also looks to the future with hope.

One day, Mary Seton insists, we will have female Shakespeares – provided women writers can find the two keys to creative freedom: fixed incomes and rooms of their own. Virginia Woolf wrote *A Room of One's Own* in 1928, and although it's a product of its time, in 2002 it resonated with me deeply – more than anything about becoming a writer ever had before.

Bright-eyed and optimistic, nineteen-year-old Antonia made a promise to herself: one day, she'd figure out a way to have enough money and a room of her own to write. This became my life's dream, the ultimate goal for my future. I even bought the merchandise – a canvas print of the purple cover of the 1945 Penguin edition of *A Room of One's Own*, and a matching purple mug. Drink morning coffee: remember life goal. Stare blankly at wall: remember life goal. I unequivocally believed that if I had those two things, I could be a writer. And if I could be a writer, I'd have a happy and fulfilling creative life. Income and a room; that was all I needed.

Almost fifteen years after first reading *A Room of One's Own*, in a strange combination of luck and tenacity and mild insanity, I now have both these things. I can support myself financially through what Virginia Woolf would calls my 'wits', and I have a room of my own to write. Money and privacy; time and space. I can hardly believe it. My chimerical dream on a canvas print and a mug actually came true. Although it hasn't been the easiest dream to make reality and I lost my focus sometimes – plus I know this may not last forever – I kept my promise to myself. Nineteen-year-old Antonia would be euphoric; I can almost see her fist-pump. She'd give everyone in this room the biggest high-five.

As I write these words, I'm sitting in a studio at the MacDowell Colony in New Hampshire. Snow falls onto my moss-covered gable roof; a fireplace crackles to my left; a grand piano collects dust to my right; my lunch in a wicker basket was stealthily delivered just ten minutes ago by a charming man named Blake. Occasionally, deer trot past the window. Inside this studio, Edward Arlington Robinson worked for twenty consecutive summers; Thornton Wilder apparently wrote *Our Town* within these very stone walls. Their names, and those of hundreds of others who've sat at this desk before me – including Australian writers Abigail Ulman and Sarah Holland-Batt – are handwritten on sixteen wooden tablets above my head. Tombstones, they call them at MacDowell. Ghosts of giants haunt this space.

There is no wi-fi or mobile reception; I don't need to cook or clean or do my son's laundry. Without any distractions or responsibilities, and with the freedom to do nothing except write, working in this studio feels like the epitome of a room of one's own. Still, something unsettles me. I thought financial independence and a room of one's own was all I needed to have a happy and fulfilling creative life. Yet in the past year since my debut novel was published, despite having those two freedoms, I still feel trapped. There've been many moments of unhappiness and frustration around what was supposed to be the fulfilment of a childhood dream. I've found Woolf's two keys to freedom, unlocked the door that opened to a room of my own, but still something isn't right.

At home a month earlier, I'd searched my bookshelf for that old pink highlighter–streaked copy of *A Room of One's Own*. I've made a mistake somewhere, I thought to myself, as I located the spine on the shelf. Where had my commitment to her battle cry gone astray? My copy of *A Room of One's Own* was now old enough to be yellow. Thankfully, after briefly panicking about the ephemeral nature of paper and how that related to my own mortality, I reminded myself it was second-hand and then felt sorry for Janet.

Perhaps I'd misunderstood Woolf, completely misinterpreted her argument to fit within my own foolish desires; I probably should glance over the essay again. Seeing my earnest handwritten notes squeezed into margins made me cringe; teenage Antonia's naive intensity was only matched by her fondness for exclamation marks. I shut the book, slightly disgusted with myself and my superfluous punctuation, and placed it into my suitcase. I would deal with my childish annotations later, when I was at MacDowell.

Unfortunately, that moment is upon me right now. I put another log on the fire and confront the book. All these shouty messages from my past-self keep distracting present-self from the text. I wish I'd written them in pencil so I could rub them out. Most of these footnotes – like 'Mussolini was a facist!' or 'The taxi is a metaphor!' – are painfully obvious. Except one:

'1928 + 100 - 2002 = 26!!!'

As I sit by the fire and stare at my mathematical scribble in the margin, I wonder what past Antonia meant by it. Typically, it seems, I'd turned *A Room of One's*

Own into a numbers game; young women are prone to such silly thoughts. Beside my addition and deduction, what else is happening on the page? Imagined Mary Seton is assessing imagined Mary Carmichael's imagined first novel *Life's Adventure*. While it was a good book, Mary Seton mused, because of then present-day constraints on the creative freedom of her gender, Mary Carmichael was no literary genius yet. I'd underlined these words: 'Give her another hundred years . . . give her a room of her own and five hundred a year . . . She will be a poet, in another hundred years' time.' Below this, I'd written another note: 'See last paragraph of book!'

I throw my legs over the side of my armchair and flick to the last page of Chapter Six, where Woolf concludes her call to arms. 'For my belief is,' she wrote, 'that if we live another century or so . . . and have five hundred a year each of us and rooms of our own; if we have the habit of freedom and the courage to write exactly what we think . . . then the opportunity will come and the dead poet who was Shakespeare's sister will put on the body which she has so often laid down. Drawing her life from the lives of the unknown who were her forerunners, as her brother did before her, she will be born.'

A hundred years after 1928, it'd be 2028. In 2002, that was twenty-six years away: what I was calculating was precisely how long we had left until the world would finally stop telling women writers they were inferior writers. What I find most striking now about my margin maths are those three exclamation marks – '!!!'. Knowing what I know about past Antonia's buoyant innocence about the big wide world, I am positive the exclamation marks meant this: 'Hurray! I'm so excited all these problems will be solved in only twenty-six years time!'

Let's recalculate for 2016:

$1928 + 100 - 2016 = 12!!!$

In just twelve years, Woolf will have written those words a century ago – and that moment in time will be upon us. Sadly, I'm considerably less excited and optimistic than I was at nineteen about this looming countdown to the 100th anniversary of *A Room of One's Own* being published. Instead, I now see those three exclamation marks as a warning.

If twelve years is all the time we have left until a writer's gender will be irrelevant to questions of their greatness, until the world will allow a woman to be Shakespeare without condemnation, time is running out. Woolf gave us a deadline and it's just around the corner. But the clock still ticks. So, if like me, you don't want Virginia Woolf to angrily or disappointedly or regretfully turn in her grave in 2028, I suggest we still have some work to do.

After rereading *A Room of One's Own* again, in my room of my own in New Hampshire, I realise how tongue-in-cheek it is; how much Woolf employs irony and paradox to invert everything she's saying and provoke us to question the status quo. All that went over my head in 2002. Woolf makes me burst into laughter with lines like this one: 'I am reminded by dipping into newspapers and novels and biographies that when a woman speaks to women she should have something very unpleasant up her sleeve,' Woolf playfully observes. 'Women are hard on women. Women dislike women . . . Let us agree, then, that a paper read by a woman to women should end with something particularly disagreeable.'

Or where she addresses the young women in the audience at Cambridge: 'May I remind you,' Woolf finger-wags, 'that in 1919 – which is a whole nine years ago – women were given a vote? May I also remind you that most of the professions have been open to you for close on ten years now? When you reflect upon these immense privileges and the length of time during which they have been enjoyed . . . you will agree that the excuse of lack of opportunity, training, encouragement, leisure and money no longer holds good.' I hadn't understood at nineteen just how much Virginia Woolf was a shit-stirrer. She is, dare I suggest it, funny. For a woman.

So, women of 2016. Let us stop looking for excuses as to why exactly the male writer is still automatically deemed superior, or why his words still sound better to our ears, or why his books are still more important. Think of how much has changed for us since 1928! How lucky I am to be born 100 years after Virginia Woolf – in 1982 instead of 1882. Women have been voting for nearly a century now – practically an eternity – and virtually equivalent to the 2500 years, since the dawn of Athenian democracy, that only men had this power.

If Virginia Woolf had money and privacy to write back in 1928, why was she still complaining? These days, many women writers across the globe have both of those too – including me. Who am I to point out any disadvantages when I'm in a position of privilege myself? After all, there are many great women writers creating works of art without a source of steady income, or in poverty, or juggling writing with demanding full-time jobs. Or without a door to close and a space to call their own, with colleagues interrupting the forming of their sentences, or partners suddenly needing to talk with them during private moments of quiet reflection, or children at their feet whingeing for as much attention as their mother gives Microsoft Word. Shouldn't we all just be thankful and shut up? Aren't there more urgent and important things we need to talk about than spare rooms and a bit of cash?

Virginia Woolf's argument is also entrenched in both the era and place in which she lived – early 20th-century England. Here in the early 21st century, the circumstances and fate of women writers have drastically improved. Today, more women are enrolled in universities than men; more books written by women are published each year than books written by men. So . . . isn't it time we put this whole 'room of one's own' conversation to bed? Obviously women are smart and can write. Maybe Janet, the previous owner of my book, already knew this – maybe that was why she gave her copy away.

Eighty-eight years after its first publication, *A Room of One's Own* still feels relevant and urgent, though. I place another log on my fire, tap my foot and stare, absent-minded, out the window of my studio. Outside, I watch the sky darken as the temperature drops. Puddles of sun-thawed snow freeze into ice sheets before my eyes. I switch on my lamp, adjust the central heating and return to the dog-eared book.

Virginia Woolf wanted women writers to have a long tradition of writing by women to read. Well, yes, we have that now. Check. She wanted us to travel – check. 'To idle, to contemplate the future or the past of the world, to dream over books and loiter at street corners and let the line of thought dip deep into the stream' – check, check, check. Independence – check. Rooms of our own – check. What more do women writers need?

I turn my gaze back to the window. Wind shakes the trees. It's cosy and warm inside my studio; it's subzero and bone-chillingly cold out there, in the woods. Compared to eighty-eight years ago, we cannot deny that today women writers do have better opportunities, training and remuneration. What of Shakespeare's sister being reborn? There are countless talented female playwrights – but perhaps that's not the point. As I read *A Room of One's Own* again, comparing the talents and abilities of Shakespeare and his imaginary sister wasn't what Woolf meant by telling us Judith Shakespeare's tragic life story. Woolf's concern for 'women of genius' like Shakespeare's sister wasn't about writing by women not being 'good enough'. What worried Woolf was how we'd create the ideal circumstances that allow for genius and creativity: circumstances unhindered by questions of the writer's sex.

For Virginia Woolf's claim that 'a woman must have a room of her own to write' was only the beginning of the greater change she sought; it was simply the first step in many more to be taken. She also wanted equal opportunity, equal voice, equal reading; they were just harder for Woolf to envision than money and a room. What seemed almost impossible in 1928, we take for granted today. Her future is our present.

I close the book and place it on my lap. Since we're comfortable inside this warm and private room, perhaps it's time we shift our attention again. To understand *A Room of One's Own* today we need to look further ahead, and carefully examine what's happening outside – in the cold, in public, on the other side of this door.

Now I'm going to ask that you jump forward with me in time. We're no longer sitting by a fire in a writer's studio in New Hampshire; it isn't snowing and there are no deer scampering across fields. We've now travelled to the opposite side of the world, to a different hemisphere, and several months have passed. Winter is over; today it is a late autumn day.

I'd like to invite you into another room. There aren't many windows so there's not much natural light, although beyond the door you can see seagulls and sunshine glimmering on the surface of the water. This room is here in Sydney, and we'll need to be very quiet and not draw attention to ourselves; we're not wearing the right lanyard so we don't really have permission to be here. We're inside the writers' festival green room, but we're flies on the wall. Don't help yourself to a finger sandwich or cup of tea, or we might get thrown out.

There are many women who also happen to be writers in the green room, although it's not of their own. It's crowded inside. But they're stuck in here until a festival volunteer comes to usher them onto their events, giving us the perfect opportunity to observe them in the wild. A disclaimer, though. I'm making things up; none of the people I'm about to introduce you to are real. None of this story I'm about to tell you is true, but that doesn't mean there aren't truths in it. Like Virginia Woolf in *A Room of One's Own*, I want us to use our imaginations to bring some kernel of reality to light. This weird activity – making stuff up – is an unfortunate quirk for which novelists like myself are at serious risk. But there might be facts in the fiction that follows.

Look over there, near the sandwiches. There's that novelist you like; you loved her last book. Her two young children are with her in the green room, helping themselves to chocolate biscuits. Across the table, someone is asking this novelist how on earth she manages to juggle something as selfless as motherhood with writing fiction. It must be so challenging and difficult to justify, they say, not to mention so hard on her kids to not always have their mother's attention. Or how boring it must be for these children to come to events like this. What the novelist wants is to throw her hot coffee and sandwiches in this person's face and yell, 'Juggle this!' – instead, she smiles, nods and agrees.

Can you see that writer to our left, sitting by herself? She's leafing through the paper but I wonder why she's frowning. Let's read over her shoulder. Oh, I see. Her short story collection has been reviewed in the books pages today; I wonder what it says. 'Trying to be ambitious . . . she has some potential as a writer . . .' Still, at least it got reviewed, even though the rest of it seems to actually be more about her novelist husband than her book, about how the marriage in one story must be based on their marriage. In a world of shrinking review pages and declining book sales, shouldn't she just be grateful that there was any coverage at all?

I bet you recognise that journalist, over in that corner. The one looking down at her mobile. Is it the phone that's making her look so green? What app is she using? Twitter. She was in the middle of composing a tweet about the panel she's on soon, but I guess got distracted by some 140-character rape threats. From someone who claims they're going to be in the audience of her event. She turns her phone off and hides it down the bottom of her bag. No wonder she looks like she's about to vomit: in a couple of minutes, she needs to get on stage.

Here's the seasoned professional sitting on the sofa. Calm, poised, twelve novels and several awards under her belt. She's been doing this for forty years. What we can't see is how much she really doesn't want to be here, how much she hates public speaking, how those old awards don't necessarily translate into new sales figures, and how unfair it feels that some of her male contemporaries aren't pressured to still hustle for book sales like this. She had so much more energy once, back in the 1970s, so much hope that one day her body of work wouldn't be read through the filter of her gender – but it's still happening in 2016.

Beside her on that sofa, there's a young writer who's just introduced herself to a famous male author. She tells him that he's one of her heroes and that his books changed her life; he tells her that dress looks great on her and why don't they have a drink later tonight. Maybe, she says, once their event together is over. He's surprised she's going to be speaking alongside him; she's so young, he thought she was a publicist. The writer and her actual publicist share an outraged look. Is that steam coming out of her publicist's ears?

Opposite them is another writer, who right now

is feeling like the only brown person in the room. She doesn't want to get on stage again and talk about diversity – again. She's feeling deflated after an earlier panel, when someone suggested her novel wasn't 'ethnic enough' because it wasn't only about suffering and hardship. Wasn't it her responsibility to make her novel more authentic, more autobiographical, they'd asked. Didn't she feel some duty to represent her people? But what point is there insisting there's diversity within diversity, she thinks, when writers of colour keep getting told that there's only one story readers want to read about race?

Uh oh, I think we've been spotted by a festival staff member. Let's leave the exclusive green room before we're escorted out. Or banned from the festival altogether.

Money and a room of one's own. Do we still think this is all that women writers need? I wish I could say that what happens externally doesn't matter; that it's all just noise. That it'd be best to ignore it. That for every writer – of any gender, background and age – the real and important work is what happens inside rooms, in private, when they're writing. External validation? Unimportant! Let's all validate ourselves!

Validation isn't the problem here, though. What I'm worried about is the effect that all this systemic, insidious, direct, oblique, conscious and unconscious sexism has on a female writer's state of mind.

Virginia Woolf worried about this too – that 'there would always have been that assertion – you cannot do this, you are incapable of doing that – to protest against, to overcome.' And that's the essence of *A Room of One's Own*: how can anyone write great literature if they're preoccupied by overcoming a hostile environment? 'All desire to protest, to preach, to proclaim an injury, to pay off a score, to make the world the witness of some hardship or grievance' – these were all obstacles in the 19th century, and in 1928, and today.

So, who's fault is all this? Who should we blame? Women themselves? Men? The industry? I'm not really interested in finger-pointing, but I think it's important to unpack some fictions we've been told.

First fiction: that biology has anything to do with cultural inequality between male and female writers. I think Virginia Woolf would've loved neuroscience. 'It is fatal,' she tells us, 'for anyone who writes to think of their sex. It is fatal to be a man or woman pure and simple; one must be woman-manly or man-womanly.' What Woolf describes has since been clarified by science: hormones, and how the balance of testosterone and oestrogen shapes the architecture of our brains. There's much chemical overlap between the sexes; men can express nearly as much oestrogen as testosterone, and women can express predominantly testosterone rather than oestrogen. Everyone has both. Instead of creating some difficult man-woman opposition, let's focus on oestrogen and testosterone – being 'woman-manly or man-womanly' – and the effect hormones might have on a writer's brain.

Oestrogen builds more nerve connections between distant regions within the brain. It is linked to an ability to collect and integrate broad amounts of information; to imagination; to abstract thought; to mental flexibility and an ability to tolerate ambiguity; to empathy; to emotional expressivity; to verbal fluency and a capacity for words; and to seeing the big picture. Oestrogen creates a mind that thinks in a web instead of straight lines, that casts its net broadly like a searchlight instead of a laser. Testosterone, on the other hand, is linked to systemising; to getting to the point; to an economy with words; to being self-confident and bold; to aggression and competition; to a desire to succeed; and to difficulties containing emotions. But the truth is, what we think we know about how oestrogen and testosterone map the brain is all still hypothesis. Perhaps these assumptions about both hormones are just another example of our bias.

Second fiction: that we are living in a literary meritocracy. That the good books will rise to the top, regardless of who wrote them. Nope. Words by women are still being read differently. Our expectations – of women as characters and women as writers – are still unattainably high for both behaviour and appearance: perfection, or else. Yet women's achievements and abilities are still given sharply lower evaluations than the achievements and abilities of men. We still scrutinise, moralise, condescend, demand proof of competence. We still underestimate the female reader. We still relegate writing for women and writing by women into categories perceived as inferior to writing by men.

These two fictions are still being treated as fact. And this has negative consequences for all writers, male and female. Hierarchies – fictional or otherwise – are dangerous. But for women writers, it has a corrosive effect. Please just give me a room of my own and then leave me alone so I can write, Virginia Woolf thought. Fair enough, I think. These rooms still exist in towns, in cities, in states, in countries, in the world, on our planet, in this universe. But the truth is, what women writers need is a universe of one's own – not just a room.

It's not enough to just point out the problems;

change doesn't happen through observation. It requires action. But if language is liquid, reading is its filter, and writing is its process of distillation, then these building blocks of culture are fluid. Culture is malleable. It can alter its state – like water – from ice to liquid to steam. Culture can be changed. We have twelve years until it's 2028; the clock still ticks but there's time. And like Virginia Woolf, I am optimistic that we can see Shakespeare's sister reborn, into a universe that will allow her to flourish.

Back in my studio in snowy New Hampshire: I sob as I read the final paragraph of *A Room of One's Own*: 'As for her coming without that preparation, without that effort on our part, without that determination that when she is born again she shall find it possible to live and write her poetry, that we cannot expect, for that would he impossible. But I maintain that she would come if we worked for her, and that so to work, even in poverty and obscurity, is worth while.'

This is not just a book about money and privacy; it's about preparation, effort, determination – solidarity and the future. *A Room of One's Own* is about addressing the truths of today and the belief that they can be changed tomorrow.

What follows truth? Dare.

So, truth or dare.

Do you dare disturb the universe?

Because I want to live in a universe where we stop discrediting women's voices. Where we stop talking about male and female styles of writing, remove the tarnish from what's considered 'feminine' and stop hollowly praising the spare and sparse – the 'masculine'.

I want to live in a universe where one woman's success isn't the exception to the rule. Or where only certain kinds of women writers are 'good writers'. Let's not pretend that our idea of 'good writing' might be shaped by thousands of years of cultural supremacy and testicular ideas about what literature should be.

I want to live in a universe where 'ambition', 'promise' and 'potential' aren't insults for women writers, said with a condescending sneer. Where women have the freedom to write whatever they please; that when they write they aren't anticipating criticism because of their gender.

I want to live in a universe where we stop Goldfinching and pandering and having that same 'if he were a woman' conversation about Jeffrey Eugenides again and again.

I want to live in a universe where women writers asserting themselves doesn't mean men need to retaliate or defend their talent or writing, because their talent and writing aren't actually being attacked.

I want to live in a universe where women writers have the option to pose for author photos without wearing makeup – or to smile, or frown, or look attractive, or not, without that photo creating a filter for how their work is read.

I want to live in a universe where a woman's work doesn't need to include a male protagonist, or war, to be considered 'serious writing'.

I want to live in a universe where biographical details of a woman's life aren't used to diminish their imagination. A universe where a woman's privacy to write is extended beyond the rooms of their own. Where, if they've revealed anything personal, they're not accused of over-sharing – which is not really writing, just self-indulgently talking about themselves. Or, if they choose to reveal nothing about themselves at all, nobody feels the need to unmask them.

I want to live in a universe where a woman writer can give a lecture, and not have someone in the audience belittle their ideas by making a comment on their appearance – negative or positive. Being a feminist and having shiny hair aren't mutually exclusive, and how someone looks shouldn't be an effective way to shut their argument down.

I want to live in a universe where literary criticism isn't taken at face value, that we critique the ways books about women or by women are critiqued, and where critical reception is an interactive cultural practice – less about classification, or where a writer and their writing fit.

I want to live in a universe where a female readership isn't considered a lesser readership. Where book clubs are seen as modern-day Greek symposiums, the forums of serious discussion about the issues of our time.

I want to live in a universe where women writers aren't told to settle down, or behave, or be quiet. Where they can shout or whisper if they want to, or swear under their breath, or loudly recite haiku.

I want to live in a universe where we stop incorrectly using the word 'sentimental' as a slur when we talk about writing that contains any emotion. In *The Art of Fiction*, John Gardner warns against sentimentality: emotion that 'rings false, usually achieved by some form of cheating or exaggeration.' Sentimentality isn't the same as sentiment, though; Gardner says 'without sentiment, fiction is worthless'. Emotion isn't hysteria.

I want to live in a universe where women writers aren't scared to get on stage and talk, in case the lady doth protest too much.

And I want to live in a universe where I can use as many exclamations marks as I want without feeling any guilt about it. And right now I will use them excessively.

1928 + 100 − 2016 = 12!!

Today my exclamation marks mean this: 'Hurray! I'm so excited all these problems will be solved in only twelve years time!'

ACKNOWLEDGEMENTS

Maraming salamat (thank you) to Cate, Mum, Dad, Julian, José, James, Eliza, Alison, Stewart, Sophie, Amy, Dave, Henry, Jemma, and especially Adolfo Aranjuez: nagpapasalamat ako at tinulungan mo ako. Special thanks to my grandmothers, Ona and Grandma, both of whom I miss very much.

PENGUIN SPECIALS

OTHER PENGUIN SPECIALS YOU COULD TRY:

From Despair to Hope	James Arvanitakis
Beauty's Sister	James Bradley
Rudd, Gillard and Beyond	Troy Bramston
Governor Bligh and the Short Man	Peter Cochrane
Fighting with America	James Curran
Utzon and the Sydney Opera House	Daryl Dellora
The Coal Face	Tom Doig
The Embarrassed Colonialist	Sean Dorney
The Absent Therapist	Will Eaves
Beyond the Boom	John Edwards
The Ellis Laws	Bob Ellis
On Listening	Martin Flanagan
The Badlands	Paul French
The Girl with the Dogs	Anna Funder
The Rise and Fall of the House of Bo	John Garnaut
The Deserted Newsroom	Gideon Haigh
End of the Road?	Gideon Haigh
The Adolescent Country	Peter Hartcher
Life in Ten Houses	Sonya Hartnett

OTHER PENGUIN SPECIALS YOU COULD TRY: CONTINUED

The Simple Life	Rhonda Hetzel
Does Cooking Matter?	Rebecca Huntley
Take Your Best Shot	Jacqueline Kent
What Would Gandhi Do?	Michael Kirby
A Wary Embrace	Bobo Lo
A Story of Grief	Michaela McGuire
The Tunnel	Dennis McIntosh
Mistakes Were Made	Liam Pieper
Ballots, Bullets and Kabulshit	Toby Ralph
Is There No Place for Me?	Kate Richards
Salad Days	Ronnie Scott
The First Dismissal	Luke Slattery
Reclaiming Epicurus	Luke Slattery
After Cancer	Dr Ranjana Srivastava
Dying for a Chat	Dr Ranjana Srivastava
You're Just Too Good To Be True	Sofija Stefanovic
A Curiosity of Doubts	TL Uglow
Condemned to Crisis?	Ken Ward